Graded Readers Series 4
edited by Eric Orton

Richard Musman

Dr. Fairbanks

illustrated by
Jim Russell

W0393516

Ferdinand Schöningh 43541

CONTENTS

Alle Rechte, auch die des auszugsweisen Nachdrucks, der fotomechanischen Wiedergabe und der Übersetzung, vorbehalten. Dies betrifft auch die Vervielfältigung und Übertragung einzelner Textabschnitte, Zeichnungen oder Bilder durch alle Verfahren wie Speicherung und Übertragung auf Papier, Transparente, Filme, Bänder, Platten und andere Medien, soweit es nicht §§ 53 und 54 URG ausdrücklich gestatten.

© 1976 by Ferdinand Schöningh at Paderborn. Printed in Germany. T.

ISBN 3-506-43541-8

Dr. Fairbanks

Chapter 1

"What's the matter now, Caro? I'd only just got to sleep."

Andrew Fairbanks turned over and pulled the sheet over his head.

"No, you don't!" Caroline said, pulling off the sheet. "The Cobleys want you. It sounds serious."

Andrew sat up. "It *must* be serious," he said. "Tom Cobley hates doctors."

"It was Mrs. Cobley who phoned. She says her husband has a terrible pain in his foot. She says he's shouting and smashing things."

"Give me the phone!"

"No! I've already said you were coming!"

Andrew dressed. He picked up his black bag, got into his new M.G. and drove off across the moors. It was raining. It was the wettest summer for years. Water poured across the road and splashed against the car. He drove up the narrow lane to the farmhouse and jumped out of his car into thick mud. Mrs. Cobley opened the door. She was like a frightened little mouse, and she spoke in a soft voice.

"He's quiet now," she said, "now that he knows you're here."

He followed her upstairs. A broken glass lay near the bedroom door. There was a pool of water on the carpet and the bedclothes were on the floor. Tom Cobley was lying at the end of the bed, holding his foot in both hands. He was a huge man, with enormous hands and a broken nose.

Andrew felt the swollen foot. Tom Cobley swore at him. "What do you think you're doing? Do you call yourself a doctor?"

Andrew turned to Mrs. Cobley. "He'll have to have a blood test. Take him to the hospital tomorrow morning for the test. Then bring him to the surgery on Friday." He gave her a bottle of pills. "Meanwhile give him these — one every four hours. They'll help to stop the pain and keep him quiet."

"I'm not taking any pills!" Tom roared.

It was then that Andrew noticed the boy. He was standing at the door. He was tall and had very fair hair and blue eyes. His shoulders were broad, but Andrew guessed that he was younger than he looked. His face was dirty, and his hair hung down his cheeks. He came and stood in front of Andrew.

"I've cut myself," he said.

He held out his right arm. He had wrapped a dirty handkerchief round it just above the wrist. Andrew took off the handkerchief and looked at the wound.

"How did you do that?" he asked.

"I fell off a rock by the river."

"Why didn't you tell me?" Sybil Cobley cried.

The boy did not answer.

"Yes. Why didn't you tell Mrs. Cobley?" Andrew asked. "That's a very nasty wound." He held up the

dirty handkerchief. "Don't you know you have to keep a wound clean? I'll have to put some stitches in your arm. You won't feel anything. I'll give you a local anaesthetic. Mrs. Cobley, will you please boil some water and bring me a clean towel?"

Andrew made the boy sit down at a table where there was a bright light. He cleaned the wound, and gave the anaesthetic. Then he took a needle and some black silk from his bag.

"Is that what you're going to sew me up with, doc?" the boy asked.

"That's right," Andrew said.

"It's like sewing up a piece of torn cloth, isn't it? It doesn't hurt at all."

"That's what a local anaesthetic is for."

When he had finished dressing and bandaging the wound, he said, "I'm going to give you an anti-tetanus injection."

"What's tetanus?"

"Ever heard of lock-jaw?"

"Yes."

"Well, that's what tetanus does. It locks your jaws together, and makes your body so stiff you can't move. What's your name?"

"Dave — Dave Cobley."

Andrew looked at Mrs. Cobley.

"He's Tom's nephew," she said quickly. "His mother died six months ago, and his father's in hospital in Bradford. He's very ill. The doctors say he won't get better."

"So you're from the north, Dave?" Andrew asked. "How do you like living on the moors?"

"I like riding in the dark —"

"That's enough!" Tom Cobley shouted. "The doctor's finished, so get to bed, boy!"

Dave did not move. Andrew picked up his bag and went to the door.

"Bring them both to the surgery on Friday morning, Mrs. Cobley."

He looked at the mousy little woman. It was difficult to imagine her at the wheel of a Land Rover. Dave still had not moved.

"How old are you, Dave?"

"Fourteen," Dave answered.

"Well, let your aunt look after you. She'll do it better than you can."

Tom swore. "Go to bed, boy! Didn't you hear me?"

As Andrew drove home, the first light was appearing above the moor. He climbed the long moorland road to the house. In two minutes he was in bed again. He pulled the bedclothes round him and went to sleep. But he woke up again at once. Caroline was climbing out of bed. Timothy, their one-year-old son, was howling.

"That's the third time tonight!" she said.

Caroline was small and fair. She liked being busy and believed that most married women have time to do a job. So she wrote magazine stories. She found people interesting, and Andrew sometimes discussed his problems with her. When she had got back into bed, he said,

"Tom Cobley's nephew's living with him. I think

they go out together on the moors — at night. What do you think they do?"

But Caroline was already asleep.

Chapter 2

Andrew and Caroline Fairbanks lived on the edge of the moor, about three miles from Dunsford. Dunsford lay in the valley below. It was a market town, but it was also a tourist centre. At holiday time the hotels were full of people who had come to explore the moors, and the riding-stables were busy all the time.

It was in this little town that Andrew Fairbanks and two other doctors had their surgery. The three men shared the practice, and so had an easier life than doctors who worked on their own. Andrew was free on Wednesday afternoons and on most Sundays. On these days he received no phone calls at night.

On Friday morning as he drove to the surgery, the sun shone in a clear blue sky. The morning mist had disappeared. A group of children were running through the heather. Ponies were eating the bright green grass on the edge of the moorland road. One of them walked across the road in front of him.

He parked his car outside the surgery. Mollie, the receptionist, welcomed him warmly. He was her favourite doctor.

"I like your new shirt," she said. "It *is* new, isn't it?"

"Yes, Mollie, it is. My wife chose it for me. Well, what have you got for me today?"

"Rather a long list, I'm afraid, doctor, and there's a new patient. He said he must see *you*."

"Dave Cobley?"

"Yes. He's come with Mr. Cobley."

"That's right. I want to see him, Mollie."

A man was swearing and groaning in the waiting-room. They looked at each other and smiled.

"He hasn't stopped making that noise since he arrived," Mollie said. "He's first on your list."

"Thank you, Mollie."

Andrew went into his room and sat down at his desk. He rang the bell. Tom Cobley came through the door with a stick in each hand. He fell into a chair and groaned.

"Well, Mr. Cobley, I've got your blood test report. You've got gout. It's a sort of rheumatism. Nothing to worry about. If you do as I tell you, it won't cause you much trouble. Get your wife to take this prescription to the chemist. Take one pill three times a day, and the swelling and the pain will soon go. Take the pills, too, if you ever start another attack. They'll stop the pain very quickly."

Tom looked at the prescription. "I'm not taking any pills! I knew someone who died from taking pills!"

"Why have you come to see me, then?"

Tom Cobley swore loudly.

"Because the blood test is no good. The foot is as bad as ever."

"Blood tests don't cure gout! If you want to get better, you'll have to take the pills."

Tom threw the prescription on the table. He moved slowly towards the door, groaning as he went.

"If you don't take those pills, you'll be sorry, Mr. Cobley."

Tom Cobley rubbed his broken nose and swore at Andrew.

"All right, Mr. Cobley! But don't expect a visit from me again in the middle of the night!"

Tom was just going out of the door, when Andrew said, "How did your nephew cut his arm, Mr. Cobley?"

Tom gave the doctor a quick, suspicious look. "He told you, didn't he?"

"Yes. But what was he doing?"

Tom Cobley raised one of his sticks and fell. He roared with pain as Andrew helped him to get up.

"I don't know what the boy was doing, do I?" he said. "I wasn't with him."

Andrew shut the door behind him and rang the bell.

A moment later Dave appeared. He was wearing a torn shirt and a pair of dirty jeans. His boots were covered in mud. Andrew noticed how pale he was.

"Well, take off your shirt, Dave."

Dave Cobley did not move. "I can't," he said.

"Why?"

"I can't lift my arm."

The doctor got up and pulled the shirt over the boy's head.

"Did you put that clean bandage on?"

"No. Aunt Sybil did."

The bandage had stuck to the wound, so that Andrew had to cut it off. The lower part of the arm was red and swollen.

"What happened this time?"

The boy looked down at the floor. "I fell off a horse."

"What!" Andrew cried. "You rode a horse with eight stitches in your arm?"

Dave was silent.

"What were you doing on the horse?"

"I can't tell you."

"Why not?"

The boy did not answer.

"Did you let your aunt know that you were going to ride?"

"No."

"But you showed her your arm?"

"I showed her it this morning, because it was hurting."

"Is she still in the waiting-room?"

"No, Tom made her drive him home."

"Well, I've got to send you to hospital."

He picked up the phone and dialled the hospital. He asked for the casualty department and spoke to the sister.

"Yes, a bed please, sister," he said. "But I don't think he'll be with you long. I'll come and see him this evening ..... Ambulance? No. He can walk."

He put down the phone and looked up. In a second he was on his feet.

Chapter 3

Andrew pulled the boy back from the door.

"I don't want to go to hospital," Dave cried. "I've seen my dad in hospital. He's been there for months and months."

"Lie down on the couch," the doctor ordered.

Then he called Mollie. "Mollie, please ring Sister Meadows and tell her that I'll want an ambulance after all. But we won't need a stretcher!"

Dave lay on the couch.

"I've got to sew your arm up again," the doctor said. "And this time I'm going to give you a penicillin injection. The wound is infected."

"Now, behave yourself in the hospital," Andrew said when he had finished, "and don't give the nurses any trouble."

"Nurses? I'd forgotten about the nurses!"

The ambulance arrived and took Dave to hospital.

It was 11 o'clock when Andrew had seen his last patient. As he was leaving the surgery, he saw Geoffrey Maxwell sitting at his desk. Geoffrey was the oldest doctor in the practice. He was not married. But he was a good doctor and Andrew often went to him for advice. They were good friends.

"Hullo, Andy!" Geoffrey said. "Come in. What can I do for you?"

Andrew sat down. "How well do you know the Cobleys, Geoff?"

"Not very well. I visited them once, a long time ago. she had a bad back, and *he* had no sympathy for her at all. In fact, he ordered me to get her back in the kitchen by the weekend!"

"Did you?"

"As a matter of fact, I did! She's a nice little woman. Does everything you tell her and never complains."

"What about Tom Cobley?"

Geoffrey Maxwell looked surprised. "He's one of the nastiest people I've met. He's lazy and dishonest. He treats his wife like dirt and he's also been to prison — for attacking a policeman."

"I didn't know that."

"It was before you came to Dunsford. He had drunk too much, and he broke the policeman's jaw. He has a frightening temper."

"Cobley's nephew, Dave, has come to live with them. He is fourteen. His mother is dead, and his father is in hospital, dying of cancer, I suppose."

"Well, I'm sorry for the kid."

"That's just how I feel. I've just sent him off to hospital with a badly infected arm. When he comes out, he'll have to go back to the farm."

Geoffrey laughed. "And you don't want him to go back! Why don't you talk to the social worker?"

"What worries me most is, the boy may *want* to go back."

"Then let him go back! You can't stop him."

"Listen, Geoff! Cobley takes the boy out on the moors at night. One day they'll get caught."

"Poaching! That's what they do," Geoffrey Maxwell said. "The police will help you, Andy. They know all about Cobley." He blew a smoke ring. "What's so special about this boy?"

"I just think he's worth helping, that's all."

Geoffrey smiled. "Helping people in trouble is one of your hobbies, Andy. But helping a boy like that needs a lot of time, and you haven't got it. You work too hard anyway. Go and talk to the social worker. She's a nice girl, and good at her job." He got up. "Sorry, Andy, but I must go."

As he went out of the surgery door, Geoffrey Maxwell said, "Be careful, Andy. Remember, you're not a detective. You're not even a social worker."

Andrew walked slowly across the square. A party of foreign tourists was just entering the church. He had three patients to visit — an old lady of eighty-seven, a five-month-old baby and a girl with a broken leg. The girl had fallen off her horse. He wrote out prescriptions for them all, sat with them for a few minutes, and promised to come again. Then he went home for lunch.

When he walked into the living-room, Caroline was sitting at her desk, typing.

"I'm sorry, darling," she said, "but I've got to get this story finished. It must go by the afternoon post. Your lunch is keeping hot in the kitchen. When you make the coffee, make a cup for me, too!" She went on typing, then stopped. "Oh! before I forget, Andy, Mrs. Cobley phoned."

Chapter 4

Andrew phoned Mrs. Cobley at once. Her voice sounded anxious. She was almost crying.

"Oh, Dr. Fairbanks!" she said. "I'm afraid of what Tom will do when Dave comes home. He says he needs the boy, and he thinks you'll keep him in hospital on purpose. I must warn you, doctor. He's got a terrible temper. He says —" Then there was silence.

"Did she put the phone down?" Caroline asked.

"Yes — or else Tom made her put it down. She was trying to warn me."

"Well, be careful, Andy. He's a dangerous man."

Four days later, Andrew sent Dave home. The boy seemed keen to go back to the farm. Andrew had so many other problems that he did not have time to worry about him much. Two days later, he and Caroline were having lunch when the telephone rang. It was Mr. Walesby of Woodlands House. He wasn't feeling well. Could the doctor call some time during the afternoon?

Andrew worked for the Health Service, but he also had a few private patients, and Mr. Walesby was one of them. Wilfred Walesby had a weak heart. Three years ago, Andrew had sent him to a doctor in London. The doctor had told him that there was no danger if he was careful. Wilfred followed the doctor's advice so well that he spent most of his time in bed. He was always finding excuses to call Andrew. He often had depressions, and this worried Andrew more than the weak heart.

"Just a minute, Mr. Walesby," Caroline said. "I'll

see if my husband is in. Are you in, Andy?" she whispered.

Andrew pushed back his chair. "Hell!" he said. "Tell him I'll come at once."

Caroline gave Mr. Walesby the message and then went with Andrew to the door.

"You know, Andy, everyone says you drive that M.G. of yours much too fast."

He laughed. "Well, I've heard stories about you and your Mini!"

Woodlands House was on the other side of Barle Moor. Andrew was driving across the moor when he saw a man and a boy walking towards him. He recognized them at once and stopped. He lowered the window.

"I see the gout's better, Mr. Cobley."

Tom Cobley pushed his broken nose through the open window. "I didn't need your pills, Dr. Fairbanks."

He swore in Andrew's face and then walked on. But he stopped when he saw Dave still standing by the car.

"Come away from there, boy. Do you hear?"

"I'm going to tell him about the girl," Dave said.

"What girl?" Andrew asked.

"A girl who's had an accident."

"There's not been an accident," Tom shouted. "The girl was asleep. Come on! Do you hear me?"

The boy did not move. "She didn't look like someone who was asleep. I told you to go and have a look."

"Told me!" Tom shouted. "Who do you think you are?"

Andrew got out of the car. "Where is she?" he asked.

The boy pointed across the moor. "Over there. It's not far away. I'll take you to her."

Without waiting, he began to walk down a narrow track across the moor.

Chapter 5

"I won't forget this!" Tom shouted.

Then he walked away quickly.

Andrew picked up his bag and followed Dave. There were places where the heather had grown across the track, and they had to push through it up to their knees. The ground was wet after the night's rain. Several times they had to jump deep pools of water.

"Are you sure you know where you're leading me?" Andrew asked.

"I know the moors better than you do, doc!"

The heather seemed to get thicker and thicker. But at last Dave pointed.

"There she is!" he said. "She must have fallen off her horse."

She was lying beside a large rock. Dave ran to her. He was excited.

"Look, doc! She wasn't riding a horse."

He held up a bicycle. The front wheel was bent.

"She must have come down that steep track, doc — on a bike! She must be mad."

The girl was lying at the bottom of the slope. Her jeans were covered in mud. Andrew was already on his knees beside her. He turned her over gently. She was unconscious, but from the position of her arms and legs, he guessed there were no serious fractures. Her nose was swollen and her right cheek was black and blue. There was a large bruise on her forehead.

"You see, I was right!" Dave said. "She isn't dead, is she?"

"No. But we've got to get her to hospital as quickly as possible. Do you know who she is?"

"Never seen her before. She must be one of the visitors."

Andrew felt her arms and legs and back. Nothing seemed to be broken. Dave looked down at her.

"She's quite small, isn't she, doc. And she's got very dark hair. Look! She's opening her eyes."

Andrew took her hand. "How do you feel?"

"My head aches," she said.

"How did it happen?"

"I don't know."

"What's your name?"

"I don't know."

She shut her eyes again.

"She's badly concussed. We must get her back to the car," Andrew said. "She's wet and cold."

He picked her up. He was glad she was so small.

"It's going to rain again," Dave said. "Look!"

A black cloud coming from the sea had covered the sun. The rain began to pour down.

"We must get started," Andrew said. "Here, take my bag."

They walked back along the track, Andrew carrying the girl and Dave the black bag. Soon the water was splashing up to their knees. Andrew, who had taken off his coat to cover the girl, was wet from head to foot. The rain beat against his face, and he could hardly see.

"Hey, doc!" Dave cried. "If I go in front, you can keep your eyes on my back."

"Good idea," Andrew replied.

"Is she still unconscious?" Dave asked.

"Yes. We must get her to hospital quickly."

"If she's one of the visitors, she might be staying at the Youth Hostel," Dave said. "But why was she alone? It's funny for a girl like that to be alone." He was silent for a while. Then he said, "You know, Tom hates the visitors. He says the moors belong to the moorland people."

"Is that why he didn't stop to help the girl?"

"No, that's not why."

"Why, then?"

"I don't know, really. But he didn't want anyone to know where we'd been."

It took them an hour to reach the road. The rain had stopped, but the sky was still dark. Andrew looked up and down the road. He couldn't see his M.G.

Chapter 6

"There's your car, doc," Dave said. "I can see the top of it. It's just the other side of the hill. I took you down a wrong turning."

Andrew's arms ached. His shoes were full of water, and his shirt stuck to him.

"I thought you knew the moors!"

"I do, doc. But the rain got in my eyes."

Andrew carried the girl slowly up the hill towards the car. Water was pouring down the sides of the road. Dave ran in front of him and opened the door of the car.

"Get in, Dave, and I'll pass the girl to you."

Dave got in and put the girl's head on his knees.

Her wet hair hung almost to the floor. Andrew got into the driving seat.

"Hold her head so that it doesn't move, but gently. That's right. I'll drive slowly."

"It's a good thing she's small, doc. There's not much room in the back of this M.G."

As Andrew started the car, the rain came down again. It was so heavy that he could hardly see the road. Suddenly the engine stopped. He tried to start it again, but without success. He put on the brakes.

"What's happened, doc?" Dave asked.

"We've run out of petrol."

"I thought doctors never ran out of petrol!"

"They don't. Somebody's emptied my tank!"

"Do you think it was *him*? He doesn't like you, doc."

Andrew did not answer. The rainstorm had passed. He looked out of the window and saw a farm at the bottom of the valley. A track led to it. He turned to Dave.

"I'm going down to that farm to see if I can get some petrol. Will you be all right?"

Dave looked down at the girl. "We'll be O.K., doc."

The farmer gave Andrew a can of petrol and lent him some blankets.

"I'll drive you back to the road, doctor," he said.

Before Andrew left the farm, he phoned the casualty ward at the hospital and told the sister what had happened. He asked her to have a bed ready.

"She hasn't moved, doc," Dave said as they drove off. "Is she really going to be O.K.?"

"I can't tell you anything yet," Andrew replied. "Now don't talk any more."

As soon as they reached the hospital, two men came out with a stretcher and carried the girl into the casualty ward. A moment later, Geoffrey Maxwell appeared at the door.

"What are you doing here, Geoff?" Andrew asked.

"Sister Meadows phoned me. She said you'd been in the rain a long time with an unconscious girl. I'll look after her. You go home and have a hot bath."

"I'm grateful, Geoff. She'll have to have an X-ray of her head, of course, but I don't think anything is broken." He turned to Dave. "Get in the front. I'll drive you home."

First he called at the surgery.

"Dr. Fairbanks!" Mollie cried. "What's happened to you? Where have you been?"

"I've just been for a walk in the rain with a girl, Mollie! That's all. I'm afraid I'll be about half an hour late for surgery. Will you ring everyone you can and let them know?"

"Of course, but —"

"Thank you, Mollie. I must rush! See you later."

Andrew got into the car and started the engine. "Are you afraid to go back to the farm, Dave?"

"No. But he'll beat me with his belt — like he did when he saw me talking to a policeman."

"Why doesn't he like you talking to policemen?"

"Because he's afraid of them."

"Are you fond of your uncle?"

"Fond of him? No. I hate him sometimes."

Andrew drove off to the Cobleys' farm. The boy seemed quite calm.

"Do you go on these midnight trips with your uncle because you're afraid of him? Does he make you go?"

"He can't *make* me go! No, I'm not afraid of him."

"Why do you go, then?"

"Because I enjoy it. It's exciting."

Andrew drove fast, the tyres screaming round every bend.

"You know, Dave, if that girl dies, they'll ask you questions, and you and your uncle will have to answer them. They will want to know what you were doing on the moor at that time. What will you say to them?"

Chapter 7

Andrew had his eyes on the road, but he knew Dave was looking at him.

"You're talking like a policeman, doc."

"If you're not careful, Dave, you'll get into serious trouble."

"I won't get into trouble. If they ask me what we were doing on the moor, I'll say I don't know. That's true. I *don't* know. When I asked him, he just got angry."

They reached the lane leading to the Cobleys' farm.

"He's locked the gate! He doesn't usually do that."

"We'll walk, then," Andrew said.

"You don't have to come," Dave said.

"I want to."

The lane was half a mile long. It was steep and narrow, and there were high banks on both sides. The trees which grew on the banks formed a tunnel of leaves.

"What animals does your uncle keep on the farm?" Andrew asked.

"Three horses and a cow. Aunt Sybil looks after the cow — and the chickens, and the vegetable garden. He never helps her. I do sometimes, when she's tired."

"What does your uncle do, then?"

"Sits at home in an armchair most of the day."

"And at night?"

Dave did not answer. He picked up a stone and threw it into the ditch.

"He's awful to Aunt Sybil," he said.

"What does he do to her?"

"He knocked her over the other night. Then he shouted at her when she cried."

"Are you fond of your aunt, then?"

"Not really. She treats me like a little kid. But she's kind."

Tom Cobley was standing at the door when they reached the farmhouse. He looked surprised to see them.

"You didn't expect us so soon, did you, Mr. Cobley?" Andrew said.

Tom Cobley drew his hand across his broken nose. "No, I didn't," he said. Then he turned to Dave. "I told you to come with me, boy."

Dave looked at his uncle. "That girl wasn't asleep. She was hurt. I wanted to go and see, but you pulled me back."

Tom Cobley took off his belt and began to swing it slowly in front of Dave. Dave did not move.

"I don't care how badly hurt she was, boy. I told you to come with me."

"Be careful how you use that belt, Mr. Cobley," Andrew said.

"Come inside," Tom Cobley shouted at the boy.

Andrew held Dave's arm. "If you want to come back with me, you can," he said.

"It's O.K., doc. I can look after myself."

Dave walked slowly into the house without turning round.

"Now get off my land!" Tom shouted. "And don't come near that boy again."

At that moment, Sybil Cobley came to the door. She looked more like a frightened mouse than ever. Even her skirt and blouse were mouse-coloured. Dave stood in the shadows behind her.

"Why do you have to shout so?" she said to her husband.

She put her arm round Dave.

"Look after the boy, Mrs. Cobley," Andrew said.

"I try to, doctor, but it's so difficult!" She started to cry.

"Don't use that belt, Mr. Cobley," Andrew said. "I'm warning you."

"And I'm warning *you*, doctor. I'll use the belt on you first if you don't get out."

Andrew did not move. "You try, Mr. Cobley," he said. "You just try!"

Tom shut the door. Andrew could hear him swearing, then there was silence. He waited a few more moments, and then walked down the lane to his car. He went home and changed, while Caroline made him a cup of coffee. He told her about meeting Dave, and about the girl. Then he hurried to the surgery. It was nearly eight o'clock before he had seen all his patients. Before leaving the surgery, he phoned the hospital. The girl was no longer unconscious, but she was badly concussed and she had a fractured cheekbone.

Caroline was sitting at her typewriter again when he got home. Sometimes he found the noise of her typewriter annoying, especially when he had had a hard day.

"I thought you'd finished your story," he said.

"I have," she said. "I was just waiting for you. Supper is ready."

Suddenly he remembered. "Walesby! He didn't phone this afternoon, did he?"

"No. You're not going to see him now, Andy! Why don't you phone him and explain?"

"No. He doesn't like answering the phone. It's his housekeeper's day off, so he'll be alone."

He picked up his bag.

"Don't let him keep you too long, Andy!"

As he shut the door, Timothy began to cry and Caroline ran upstairs.

*

Chapter 8

Andrew drove fast along the moorland road. But he wasn't really worried. Wilfred Walesby hadn't had a heart attack for several years. He lived alone in a large red brick house in the middle of a wood. A housekeeper looked after him. Andrew knew that he had once been married. He knew that his wife had died a few months after a child was born. But Mr. Walesby never spoke about his family. He seemed to be without friends and relations. His only companions were his cats.

Mr. Walesby had dozens of cats. On cold days, when all the windows were shut, the smell of cats sometimes made Andrew feel sick. He wanted to push them away

when they rubbed against his legs, or jumped on his knees. But he was careful not to hurt Mr. Walesby's feelings. The cats were the only thing that could make him smile. Andrew was one of the few people who ever visited him, and the only letters he received were bills.

"He's very kind," the housekeeper told Andrew, "but he can't talk about anything except his health — and the cats, of course."

Andrew had spoken to her only the week before. "It's funny," she had said, "but this morning I found a photograph of a girl on his desk. There has never been any photograph there before. I didn't dare ask him who it was."

"Why not?" Andrew had asked.

"Oh, I couldn't ask him questions like that. He won't talk about himself. You see, he came here to forget. But if you ask me, he spends all his time remembering!"

It was dark when Andrew reached the main gate. He drove slowly through the damp woods to the house. He had never liked these woods. He turned the last corner, and the house was in front of him.

There was no light on anywhere. Every window was black. He jumped out of the car. He tried the front door and the back door. They were both locked. He shouted. There was no answer. He shouted again. The only sound was the rain dripping from the leaves. There was a moon, and he could see Mr. Walesby's bedroom window. It was open.

"He's gone to bed early," Andrew thought. "I'll phone the housekeeper in the morning."

He was just getting into his car again, when he heard a noise. It got louder and louder.

Chapter 9

The moon was bright, and Andrew could see the cats rushing towards him. They miaowed and rubbed themselves against his legs. He knew that Wilfred Walesby never let his cats stay out after dark. He always stood at his front door, calling them until every one was inside. Then he fed them and locked them up in the big room downstairs.

Andrew ran to the back of the house, and the cats came running after him. He tried all the windows and at last found one which was not fastened. He climbed in. He was in the kitchen. The cats jumped in after him, screaming and miaowing when he trod on them in the dark. At last he reached the door and switched the light on. He ran down the passage and into the big room, switching on the lights as he went. A jug of milk and two cups stood on the table by the window. The cups were clean. He went into the hall and turned on the light.

Wilfred Walesby was lying on his face at the foot of the stairs. There was a cat on his back, and another was rubbing itself against his forehead. Andrew pushed the cats away and turned him over. There was a bruise on his forehead and a little blood, but Andrew knew that he was dead. The eyes that looked up at him did not move. He felt his heart. It had stopped beating. The hands were quite cold. Except for the bruise on the forehead, Andrew could find no other wound. Mr. Walesby had been dead for many hours. He rang the police. Twenty minutes later they arrived, a policeman in uniform and a detective whom Andrew hardly knew.

2 Dr. Fairbanks 43541

"Those cats!" the detective said. "I nearly broke my neck! Good evening doctor. Where's the body?"

Andrew showed him, while the policeman stood at the door.

"Is this where you found the body, doctor?"

"Yes. He was lying on his face. I turned him over to see if he was still breathing."

"You'll excuse me, doctor, but I have to ask you this question. Why are you here?"

"I'm his doctor. He phoned me during the early afternoon, saying he didn't feel well. Unfortunately I had to deal with an accident on the way. So I got here too late. It's his housekeeper's day off, so he was alone."

"Were you surprised to find him dead?"

"Yes and no. He had often told me he felt ill when there was nothing wrong with him at all. But he did have a weak heart."

"So you think he died of a heart attack?"

"It's very probable, but, of course, there'll have to be a post-mortem."

"There's nothing that makes you suspicious about his death? What about that bruise on his forehead?"

"He got that bruise when he fell."

"How long has he been dead?"

"About six or seven hours."

The detective looked down at the body of Wilfred Walesby. "You know, it's strange," he said. "There's a look of disappointment on his face. Or am I seeing something that isn't there?"

"He was an unhappy man," Andrew said.

"I'm not surprised," the detective said, looking round him.

"Have you brought the van?" Andrew asked.

"Yes." The detective turned to the policeman. "Go and get the stretcher, Snowy, and bring a blanket."

The policeman returned in a minute and they lifted Wilfred Walesby on to the stretcher. Andrew covered him with a blanket. The black cat jumped on to the stretcher and began to miaow. The detective pushed it off. While the two men carried the stretcher to the van, Andrew went into the big room. It was dusty and smelt of cats. He went straight to the desk. The photograph was still there. He picked it up.

Chapter 10

It was the photograph of a girl. She had a wide mouth and a rather small nose. She was smiling. She looked the sort of girl who knew how to look after herself. The detective came into the room and Andrew showed him the photograph. "Do you recognize her?"

The detective shook his head and called the policeman. "Ever seen this girl, Snowy?"

"Never. She can't live in Dunsford. She's the sort of girl people remember. She's probably a visitor."

Andrew put the photograph back on the desk.

"Will you want to see me again?" he asked the detective.

"We'll want a written report about Mr. Walesby if you don't mind, doctor. I'm afraid it's necessary, because you found the body. I'll come and see the housekeeper tomorrow. We'll have to find a home for all these cats."

Andrew drove home in the rain. Caroline was lying on the sofa, reading a book.

"I thought you were never coming! You look tired. Andy, is something the matter?"

He sat down beside her. "Wilfred Walesby was dead when I arrived."

"How awful! What did he die of?"

"A heart attack, I think. But we'll have to wait for the post-mortem. It's a pity I didn't get there sooner."

"You're not suggesting that Mr. Walesby's death was your fault, are you, Andy? If so, you mustn't."

He started to get up, but Caroline put an arm round him.

"Don't move," she said. "I'll bring you your supper on a tray."

Andrew was asleep before the supper arrived. Caroline woke him up.

"Come on, Andy! Here's your supper!"

The next morning when Andrew went to the hospital, the girl was still not well enough to talk. It was only on the third day that she could remember her name — Jennifer Walesby. She was eighteen, and she was spending a holiday with some young friends in a cottage not far from Torberry. The friends had got tired of the rain and had gone home. She had stayed behind in the cottage alone.

"Do you think Jennifer Walesby and the girl in the photograph are the same person?" Caroline asked.

"They don't look alike," Andrew replied.

The following day he received news of the post-mortem on Wilfred Walesby. Mr. Walesby had died of a heart attack on September 15th at about 3 o'clock in the afternoon.

Andrew drove to the hospital after surgery, as he did every morning. Jennifer was lying down when he entered the ward. Her head rested on a pillow and she did not move. Andrew sat down beside the bed.

"Hullo, Jennifer. The sister says you're much better."

"Please sit where I can see you. It hurts when I turn my head."

He moved his chair to the end of the bed. Jennifer said nothing. She was very pale, and he guessed she was pale even when she was well. Her grey eyes moved restlessly round the bed. Her dark hair was spread over her pillow.

"Are you looking at my swollen nose," she said at last.

He laughed. "It won't remain swollen for long. How are you feeling?"

"My head still hurts a bit. Otherwise I'm O.K. How long have I got to stay here? I hate staying in bed."

"Well, you'll have to stay here a bit longer, I'm afraid. Tell me, Jennifer, what were you doing on the moor on a bicycle?"

"I wanted to get somewhere. On the map the track looked much shorter than the road."

"You don't know the moors, then!"

"No, I certainly don't!"

"Why did you stay behind in the cottage when your friends went home?"

"There was something I wanted to do."

There was a silence.

"Do you live at home, Jennifer? Do your parents know —"

"I haven't got a home," Jennifer said. "My mother died when I was eight months old, and my father just disappeared. My aunt looked after me until I was sixteen. Then I got a job as a waitress."

"Did you leave your aunt, then?"

"Yes. I wanted to look after myself. I was earning enough money. A girl-friend offered me a bed in her room."

"Don't you see your aunt any more?"

"Yes. I go to see her sometimes. She misses me, I think."

A nurse passed carrying a pillow. She smiled at Andrew. A mother on the other side of the ward bent over her small daughter and kissed her good-bye. The old lady in the next bed was talking in her sleep.

"Jennifer," Andrew said. "Who were you going to see when you were cycling across the moor?"

Chapter 11

Jennifer looked surprised. "Why do you want to know?"

"It's important that I know."

"Well, it's rather a long story. I met someone in the village who told me there was a Mr. Walesby living in a house across the moor. Walesby's not a common name, so I looked him up in the telephone book. His first name began with a 'W'. My father's name was Wilfred."

She lifted her hand to her head, but let it drop on the bed again. Andrew said nothing.

"I thought a lot about it. I didn't really care whether my father was alive or dead. But I wanted to know. So next day, when everyone was packing to go home, I phoned W. Walesby from the village phone-box. When he answered the phone he didn't say anything. But I asked him a lot of questions — where he came from, whether he had a family, and so on. He almost put the phone down, but I made him listen. I told him my name was Walesby. He said he didn't want to hear any more. Then I told him I was probably his daughter."

"What did he say?"

"He didn't answer at first. I could hear him breathing heavily. Then he said he'd never had a daughter. So I told him the story of my life. I could still hear him breathing, but he didn't say a word. Then I said I was going to visit him one afternoon, and I said I'd send him my photograph. Before he could say 'no', I put down the phone."

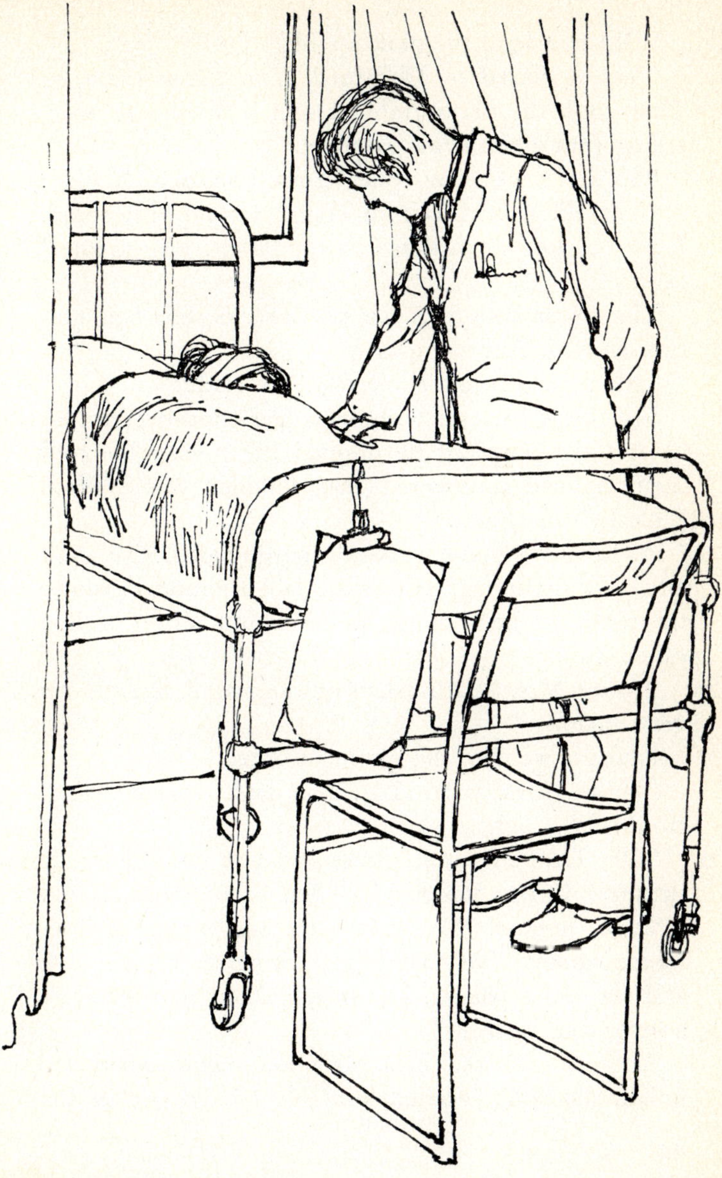

"Did you send the photograph."

"Yes, I cycled to Dunsford. You know Bailey's? They took the photograph. I sent it to him at once, telling him when I was coming."

"So that's why you rode across the moor?"

"Yes, I'll go and see him when I get out of hospital. I want to know whether he's my father. It'll be interesting."

There was colour in her pale cheeks. She was getting excited. Andrew got up.

"It's time you had some rest," he said.

She closed her eyes without saying good-bye. Before he left the hospital, he phoned the police. He told them he had discovered that Jennifer was Wilfred Walesby's daughter.

As he drove home, it began to rain again. The wind was blowing fiercely. A tree had fallen, almost blocking the road. As he shut the door behind him, Caroline called him.

"Andy, Mrs. Martindale is on the phone. She sounds very anxious."

Andrew went to the phone at once.

"Hullo, Mrs. Martindale," he said. "What's the trouble?"

"Oh, Dr. Fairbanks, please can you come and see Bridget? I'm so worried" — She was almost crying. "Please, doctor! We know you and we trust you. Please come! I've taken her temperature. It's 104, and she has a pain in her side. I thought it was just a fever, but now —"

Andrew knew that Mrs. Martindale never called him unless she really needed him. He looked out of the window. The rain was beating against the glass. The house shook beneath the wind.

"All right, Mrs. Martindale," he said. "I'll come at once."

"I'll make you some sandwiches," Caroline said.

He looked at the floor round her desk. It was covered with sheets of paper.

"I've got plenty of time," she said. "They don't want my story until Monday. Anyway, I'm not going to let you go out with an empty stomach!"

Chapter 12

As Andrew drove across the moor, the rain began to fall more heavily than ever. The Martindales lived at Havercombe, a small village not far from the coast. They worked at the Bridge Hotel, where Mrs. Martindale was a cook and her husband a waiter. Their cottage was next to the hotel.

The road to Havercombe had more bends and more steep hills than any other road in the district. Water rushed down the ditches. The bridge across the River Mellow was almost under water, and there were places where the river had burst its banks. Up on the moors, the wind nearly blew Andrew's car off the road.

Havercombe lay in a deep valley. As Andrew drove down the steep, narrow road, he could hear the roar of the River Trenthorn. He came round the final bend and put on his brakes just in time. The road as far as the bridge was covered by flood water. He left the car on high ground and got out.

To get to the Bridge Hotel he had to cross the river. He looked at the flood water. It was moving fast, but it did not look too deep. He took off his shoes and socks, pulled up his trousers, and walked into the flood. The flood water pushed him along and he reached the bridge without too much trouble. He put on his shoes and socks again and in a few minutes he was walking past the Bridge Hotel. Dick Martindale ran out of his cottage to meet him.

"Oh, Dr. Fairbanks! I'm terribly sorry! We were so worried about Bridget that we quite forgot to warn you about the flood."

"Well, Dick, I'm not very wet — just the bottom of my trousers."

"Bridget's sleeping now, doctor, but she's very hot and her breathing frightens us. What do you think's the matter with her?"

"I can't tell you anything until I've seen her, Dick."

The water was still dripping off him as he climbed the stairs. Dick took him into the bathroom and gave him a towel. He washed and dried himself. He could hear Dick walking up and down the passage.

"I won't be a minute, Dick," he called.

The mother and father were waiting for him at the bedroom door. They went in with him. Bridget was lying on her side. She was breathing with difficulty. He turned her over gently and woke her up. She began to cry and put her hand to her side.

"It hurts," she said.

Her mother took her hand. "The doctor's going to make you better, darling."

"That's right, Bridget," Andrew said. "I'm going to make you quite well, and your side won't hurt any more. Now, be a good girl and open your mouth. I'm going to put the thermometer under your tongue."

Her temperature was 105. He examined her chest. He didn't show that he was worried. He just said, "She's got pneumonia."

"Is that dangerous, doctor?" Mrs. Martindale asked.

"No, don't worry. It's not dangerous these days. There are drugs that'll cure it. But she'll have to go to hospital. Are the roads clear this side of the valley, Dick?"

"They're clear for about five miles. But there are floods between here and the Mellow valley bridge."

"Then I'll phone the city hospital. There won't be any floods between here and the city.

"But the city's miles away!" Mrs. Martindale cried.

"That means you won't be able to look after her. We do want you to look after her!"

"Try not to worry, Mrs. Martindale. The road to Dunsford is blocked. The city is much easier to reach and the hospital is excellent. Bridget will get much better treatment there than I can give her. Now can I use your phone, please?"

He went downstairs and into the living-room. He was much more worried than he had told them.

Chapter 13

Andrew shut the living-room door and phoned the city hospital.

"Can I speak to the duty doctor, please?"

While he was waiting he began to write a letter to the hospital. He had almost finished it, when he heard the duty doctor's voice at the other end of the line.

"There's a child here with pneumonia and pleurisy," he said in a low voice. "Have you got a bed free? .... Good! I can't send her to Dunsford Hospital because all the roads are blocked. ..... Yes, floods. ..... A bed in the Margaret Ward? Thank you ..... Yes, I'll give her a penicillin injection now ..... Oh! I'd like the mother to accompany her. Can you put her up? ..... You can? Fine! I'll phone for an ambulance at once. Thank you very much. Good-bye."

After phoning for the ambulance, he returned to the bedroom.

"The ambulance will be here in about half an hour.

If you want to go with Bridget, Mrs. Martindale, you can stay at the hospital. It will help Bridget if you are with her."

"Oh, thank you, Doctor Fairbanks! Of course I'll go."

While the mother held her hand, Andrew gave Bridget a penicillin injection. She gave a little cry, but was too ill to feel much pain. She continued to breathe with difficulty. He looked at her hot little face. He had brought her into the world during his first year at Dunsford. When the mother had packed a suitcase, she came and sat by the bed. Andrew left her and went to find Dick Martindale. He was sitting in the kitchen, with his face in his hands.

"It's worse than you said, isn't it, doctor?" he said, looking up.

"Yes," Andrew replied, "but you mustn't worry too much, and don't frighten your wife. There are drugs which can deal with most illnesses these days. Bridget isn't going to die! I'll just finish this letter, then your wife can deliver it at the hospital."

"I wish you were looking after her," Dick said. "We trust you."

"You can trust the doctors at the city hospital, too, Dick. They'll give her everything she needs."

There was a short silence.

"Well, how are things at the hotel?" Andrew asked at last.

"Oh, as dull as usual, you know — except when Tom Cobley came into the hotel the other day."

"Tom Cobley?" Andrew said. "What was he doing here?"

"He came to see a guest, a very rich gentleman who was staying the week-end at the hotel."

"Do you know why he came to see this guest?"

"No. But the meeting was very short! The gentleman was extremely angry. He took Tom to the door and pushed him out. Then he came back and ordered another whisky!"

"Had you ever seen this man before?"

"Never! He only stayed two nights. But I can remember his name. It was Oakley. He arrived in a blue Rolls Royce, which he drove himself."

"What was he like?"

"He was rather short, and he had a little grey beard. I think he and Tom knew each other quite well."

The ambulance arrived and took the mother and child away. Andrew looked at his watch. It was nearly 4 o'clock.

"I must go, Dick. Your wife will be able to phone you and let you know how Bridget is."

They were standing at the door of the cottage. A mist had fallen, covering the tops of the hills. They could only just see across the river. "I can't go back the way I came, Dick. I can't walk against the flood. I'll have to borrow a car."

"You can borrow mine, doctor. It's only a Volkswagen, but —"

"A Volkswagen will be fine. How can I avoid the floods?"

"Try the little road through the woods. It climbs away from the river almost at once. There's a bridge across the Mellow about fifteen miles away, but there's not enough water up the moors to start a flood. You'll get through."

Andrew climbed into the Volkswagen.

"Don't worry about Bridget, Dick. She'll be all right. Try and get a good night's sleep!"

As Andrew passed the hotel, he noticed a blue Rolls Royce in the car park. Dick had not mentioned that Mr. Oakley had returned, but then, Dick hadn't been back to the hotel that afternoon. Andrew drove on, and almost at once passed a man walking at the side of the road. He looked in his mirror. The man was short, and had a little beard. Round the next bend, a Land Rover was parked under a tree. Andrew put on his brakes. Tom Cobley was in the driving seat, with his head on his chest. He was asleep, and there was nobody with him.

As Andrew drove on, he looked again in his mirror and saw that Mr. Oakley had stopped on the other side of the road. Andrew kept his eye on the mirror until he reached the next bend. He just had time to see Oakley walk across the road to the Land Rover.

He drove up the hill. It had stopped raining and the wind was not as fierce as it had been. He reached home sooner than he had expected.

Caroline looked at the Volkswagen. "What have you done with the M.G., Andy?"

"I had to leave it on this side of the river. The floods were too deep. Dick Martindale lent me his car."

At that moment Timothy began to cry.

"Oh, no!" Andrew said. "Does he ever stop crying?"

"He's been good all day. Pick him up, darling, while I get the supper."

Andrew picked up his son, who howled louder than ever.

"He's suspicious of me, you know! I think he knows I'm a doctor."

The next morning when he reached the surgery there were fifteen patients on his list. He pressed the bell. His first patient was a boy who came to Andrew at the beginning of every term. He hoped to persuade the doctor that he was not well enough to go to school. Andrew said what he always said, "There's nothing wrong with you, Mike! You'll just have to put up with it."

He was just going to ring the bell for his second patient, when suddenly Mollie opened the door.

"I'm sorry, Dr. Fairbanks," she said. "I tried to get him to wait, but he was too strong for me."

"Not Tom Cobley?" he said.

Chapter 14

It was not Tom Cobley. It was Dave. He tried to push past Mollie, but she took his arm.

"Thank you, Mollie," Andrew said. "You can let him come in."

Dave closed the door and stood in front of Andrew.

"I've run away," he said. "I've left the farm, and I'm not going back."

"Why," Andrew said, putting his hands behind his head. "Did your uncle beat you?"

"Yes. But it's not only that."

"What is it, then?"

"He doesn't take me on those trips any more."

They looked at each other across the desk. The boy was dirty from head to foot. His shirt was hanging out of his trousers, and he wore no shoes. He lifted his right foot.

"He took them from me — to stop me from running away."

Andrew got up. Dave moved back towards the door.

"I know you think Tom and I went poaching," he said. "Well, we did. Tom had a net, and we caught trout and salmon. Sometimes he shot a deer. I helped him. I knew it was wrong, but I enjoyed it."

He stopped, but Andrew said nothing.

"He said he didn't trust me," Dave went on, "not after I helped you rescue that girl. He started locking me in my room. Yesterday I tried to climb out of the window, but he caugh tme. He beat me with his belt —"

"Show me," Andrew said.

Dave lifted his shirt. The whole back was covered with bruises. It was black and blue.

"You'll have to show this to the police, Dave."

"No! I won't go to the police."

"What do you expect me to do, then?"

"I thought you could help me."

Andrew looked down at the long list of his patients.

"I'll do what I can, Dave. Come back here at 2.30." Dave did not move. "You know what will happen to you if you don't go back to the farm?" Andrew went on. "You'll probably have to live in a 'home' with a lot of other boys."

Dave still did not move. "I'm not going back, doc."

Andrew got up. He gave Dave a five-pound-note. "Go and get yourself some shoes, and something to eat. Come back at 2.30."

He took the boy to the door. Then he phoned the social worker.

"I agree with you," she said. "The boy mustn't go back. Bring him round to me this afternoon."

Andrew put down the phone. Most of his patients that morning had nothing wrong with them. He was less polite to them than usual. One large woman was very angry with him when he told her she had put on too much weight.

"Are you suggesting I'm fat, doctor?"

His last patient left him at 11.30. The sun was shining as he drove to the hospital. He went first to Jennifer Walesby's ward.

"How do you feel, Jennifer?" he said, sitting down by her bed.

"Better. When can I get up?"

"You're lucky that the fracture is so small. But we can't let you get up yet. Anyway, what are you going to do when you leave hospital?"

"Go back to London and look for another job, I suppose. I'm fed up with the restaurant. I'll probably get a job abroad. My boy-friend won't like that!"

She smiled at last.

"Jennifer," Andrew said. "Wilfred Walesby died on the day you were going to see him. And he *was* your father."

"Oh, no!" Jennifer said. Then after a while she went on, "But you can't expect me to be sad, can you? I didn't know him, and I never thought much about him until I came here. What did he die of?"

"He had a heart attack."

"Did you know him?"

"He was my patient."

"What sort of man was he?"

"Very quiet. He never saw anybody. He spent most of his time reading."

"And he never talked about his family?"

"No, never."

"My aunt never forgave him, you know, for running away when my mother died. She says that my mother and father were much more fond of each other than they were of me."

"Did he give your aunt enough money to look after you?"

"No, he didn't. He didn't leave her anything. He just disappeared. I wonder if he got the photograph I sent him?"

"Yes, he did. I found it on his desk after he died. And there was a tea tray with two cups on it. So he was waiting for you."

"Well, I'm sorry I didn't see him. I'm sorry he's dead."

She was silent. Andrew got up.

"I'll come and see you tomorrow. Do you want us to phone your aunt about you, or your boy-friend?"

"No, thank you."

Her eyes were closed. She looked tired and lonely.

Andrew had two more patients to see at the hospital. When he got home, Caroline was interviewing someone on the telephone. She had Timothy on her knee and was finding it difficult to write notes. He took the child from her and went into the garden. The grass on the lawn was too long. He never had time to cut it. The flower beds were in a mess. The storm had blown down hundreds of apples.

He went indoors. Caroline had finished her interview.

"I think Jennifer's going to be rich," Andrew said. "People are saying that her father saved a lot of money."

"What will she do with it?" Caroline asked.

"I don't know. I don't really know what she's like, but she's an interesting kid."

Chapter 15

Dave was reading magazines in the waiting-room, He was wearing a pair of new shoes. He put his hand in his pocket and gave Andrew the change from the five pound note.

"Didn't you bring anything with you?" Andrew asked.

"I didn't have time."

"I've spoken to the social worker. She'll look after you. Come on! We'll go and see her now."

Dave followed Andrew into the street.

"What's the social worker like?" he asked. "Is she young?"

"Yes. You'll like her. Everyone does."

They walked in silence across the town. There were crowds of people in the main street. It was market day. An old lady stopped Andrew and began to tell him about her rheumatism.

"Come to the surgery tomorrow and tell me all about it," Andrew said.

Suddenly he noticed that he had lost Dave. He searched among the crowd, but could not see the boy anywhere. He waited for a few minutes, but Dave did not appear. He went at once to the police station.

"The boy's run away," Andrew said. "I think he's suspicious of the social worker. He probably thinks she's a sort of policewoman. What do you think he'll do? He's got no money."

"He'll find plenty of places to hide," the police sergeant said, "but he'll have to steal when he wants to eat. I'll tell my men to keep their eyes open, doctor."

Before he left the police station, he phoned the social worker. She laughed.

"He sounds an interesting boy! Let me know when they find him."

Andrew went home. Caroline was in the garden with Timothy.

"Well?" she said. "You don't look very cheerful, Andy!"

"I'm not! This time the boy's run away from *me*."

"I expect he wants to keep his freedom, poor kid."

"Well, I can't worry about him this afternoon. I've ten patients to visit."

"Andy," Caroline said. "You're working too hard. Why don't you go fishing one day? You haven't been for weeks."

"If it's fine on Sunday, I will," Andrew replied.

It was fine on Sunday, and Andrew went to his favourite pool on the River Mellow. The pool lay in a deep valley. As he walked down the path through the trees, he could see the sunlight on the water below him. The river was full after the heavy rain, and the water was higher in the pool than he had ever seen it. A good day for fishing! He left his sandwiches out of the sun on a high rock. Then he climbed down to the pool.

Almost at once he caught a small salmon. He was just putting it in his bag, when there was a splash in the water in front of him, then another, and another, all in the same place. He looked round. Dave Cobley was standing on top of the rock, looking down at him.

"I didn't think there were any salmon left in this

part of the river," he said. "I thought Tom and I had caught them all. You're a good fisherman, doc — but it's easier to catch them in a net!" He spoke with his mouth full. "They're good, these sandwiches. Your wife must be really O.K. Don't worry! I'll leave you a few."

"Are you the person who's helping himself to milk bottles and food from other people's homes?"

"Yes. I have to keep myself alive, don't I?"

"True! But not by stealing. Some of the people you took food from are poor. Did you know that?"

Dave did not answer.

"Why don't you go to the police before it's too late? They'll help you."

Dave still said nothing.

"Well, they'll catch you sooner or later. You won't be able to live like that when the winter comes. You don't know what the moors are like in winter."

"Yes, I do. There are moors up in the North, and it's colder up there."

"How did you know I was here?"

"*He* told me once. He told me you came here often on Wednesday afternoons and on Sundays. There's not much he doesn't know about the Dunsford fishermen."

Dave pushed a whole sandwich into his mouth.

"Did you come here just for the sandwiches?"

"Of course I didn't, doc!"

"Why, then?"

"Because — well, I wanted to talk to someone."

"Why don't you talk to the sergeant at the police station? He'll help you."

"That's what you think! He'll lock me up."

"No, he won't. He'll take you to the social worker."

"Good-bye, doc! Thanks for the sandwiches."

Andrew watched him disappear among the trees. A cloud had covered the sun. A cold wind blew down the valley. It was beginning to rain again. He packed his things and climbed the steep path to the road. As he approached the car, he saw that someone was sitting in the driving-seat. He was only five metres away when Dave jumped out.

"Get back in, Dave. You can come home and have tea with us."

"And stay the night?"

"If you like."

They looked at each other, each wondering what the other would do.

"The next day, you'll take me to the police station and the social worker, won't you, doc?" Dave said at last.

Andrew did not answer. Dave ran into the woods.

As Andrew drove home, he saw a helicopter flying slowly over Barle Moor. It was about a mile away. For a moment, Andrew thought it was going to land. But suddenly it flew away towards the sea.

Chapter 16

The following week, Jennifer Walesby came to see Andrew. Her nose was no longer swollen, and the bruise on her cheek had almost disappeared. She looked cheerful, but she was as pale as ever. She was wearing a pair of old jeans, and a shirt open at the neck. Her dark hair fell to her shoulders. At last she look ed like the girl in the photograph.

Andrew took her to his private surgery and they sat down.

"I'm sorry we can't go into the living-room at the moment. My wife's working there. She's finishing a story. She writes for a magazine."

"Really?" Jennifer said. "But I won't keep you. I've only come to thank you."

"That's nice of you. But you must thank the boy, not me. He found you."

"Where can I find him?"

Andrew laughed. "In the woods, on the moor, in the town! He's run away from his uncle and aunt, and nobody knows where he's hiding. The police are searching for him."

"Has he done anything bad?"

"No, but he thinks he has. He's frightened of the police. I'll make you some coffee."

A few moments later he came back with the coffee. "It's only Nescafé. I hope you don't mind!"

"I drink it all the time!" Jennifer said.

"Have you seen your father's solicitor yet?" Andrew asked after a short silence.

She looked at him. Her pale face became pink, and

she began to laugh. She laughed so much that she upset her coffee.

"Oh, I'm sorry!" she said. "Let me get a cloth."

"No, don't worry about that," Andrew said. "Did I say something funny?"

"Well, I think it's funny. Perhaps you won't. You see, my father phoned the solicitor the day before he died and told him he wanted to change his will. He said he wanted to leave everything to me. But, of course, it was too late. He died before the solicitor could see him."

She began to laugh again so loud that Caroline ran in.

"What's happened?" she said.

"Well, I know it's awful to laugh, but my father left everything he had to a cats' home in Torberry!"

"You mean he didn't leave you anything at all?" Caroline cried.

"Not a penny!" Jennifer said. "But I don't mind. We didn't know each other, did we?" She got up. "I must go."

"Are you going back to London?" Caroline asked.

"No. The weather's so lovely at last. I'm going to stay at the cottage for a while."

They all went to the front door. A bicycle lay on the grass outside.

"Another bicycle?" Andrew said. "And it looks like an old one."

Jennifer smiled. "I haven't enough money to buy a new one. But the cats have, haven't they?"

"Well, be careful," Andrew said. "Remember you've had concussion."

She waved good-bye and rode off down the road. Andrew saw a car coming towards her very fast. It was in the middle of the road. There was a scream of brakes. He could not see Jennifer, but the car was in the ditch. Andrew ran down the road.

Chapter 17

The car had just missed Jennifer. She had thrown down her bicycle and, like Andrew, was running towards the scene of the accident. She got there first. Andrew heard her say, "Are you all right?" A man's voice answered, "Yes, young lady. Don't worry. I won't report the accident to the police."

"I'm not worrying," Jennifer said. "It was your fault, not mine."

"No, young lady. Let me correct you. You were in the middle of the road. If I wanted to, I could make you pay for the damage to my car. But as I've said, I won't say anything to the police."

Andrew stood beside Jennifer. He recognized the man at once. He was about fifty and had a neat grey beard. It was Oakley, and the car was a blue Rolls Royce.

"I saw what happened," Andrew said. "The girl's right. You were in the middle of the road, not her. And you were certainly driving much too fast."

"Who are you?" the man asked. He sounded anxious.

"I'm a doctor. Come on! I'll help you out of the car."

"I can't move," the man said.

"I thought you said you were all right."

"I think I've dislocated my left shoulder."

Andrew opened the car door. "Come on! Push yourself along the seat. We'll catch you if you fall ..... Fine! ..... Now stand up and let's look at your shoulder. Yes, it's dislocated all right."

"Will you please put it back as quickly as possible? I'm in a hurry."

"It'll hurt," Andrew said. "You'll need an anaesthetic."

"No, no! I don't want an anaesthetic. Just put it back."

"Help me take off his coat, Jennifer."

Then with one quick movement he put the shoulder back. The man gave a cry of pain.

"It'll be rather sore for a while," Andrew said. "I'll get you a sling. You mustn't drive."

"I must get on," the man said. "Could you phone a garage, please?"

Andrew fetched the sling, while Caroline phoned the garage.

Oakley let Andrew fix the sling round his arm, but he refused Andrew's invitation to come inside and rest. He walked up and down the road until the garage man came with his van. The van pulled the Rolls out of the ditch. Oakley wrote a cheque and gave it to the garage man. Then he turned to Andrew.

"Thank you," he said.

"That's all right," Andrew replied.

Oakley climbed into the car. He could not hide his pain, but he managed to get the Rolls moving.

"It's lucky the Rolls drives itself!" the garage man said. "He'll manage all right with one hand."

Jennifer got on her bicycle again, and they watched her ride away.

"What's that man doing on the moors in a big Rolls Royce?" Caroline said. "And why did he refuse to come into the house. It seems strange to me."

Andrew brushed the dust off his trousers. "Don't ask me," he said. "I'm a doctor, not a detective."

"I'll get lunch," Caroline said. "But you won't mind if it's very simple, will you? I must get my story finished by tonight."

Timothy began to cry. Caroline laughed.

"Which do you prefer, Andy — Timothy's howling, or my typewriter?"

Andrew went into the kitchen and cut himself a thick slice of bread and cheese. He ate it sitting on the kitchen table. Then he opened a can of beer. Timothy was still crying when he had finished.

"Caroline, my love, having trouble? Well, you won't have to get my lunch. I've had it! Bye!"

"I'm sorry, darling. It's his teeth."

As he drove along, he wondered where Oakley had gone. The man was certainly in a hurry, and he had looked anxious and worried. Suddenly Andrew noticed that he was passing Woodlands House. He turned round and drove up to the front of the building. All the windows were closed. There was no sign of life. Even the cats had gone. He was just getting out of the car when he heard someone approaching behind him. He turned quickly.

Chapter 18

"Hullo, doc!" Dave said.

Dave looked thinner, and his clothes were torn.

"Is this where you're hiding?" Andrew asked.

"Yes. I found the larder window open at the back of the house. I sleep in a real bed! But you mustn't stay here, doc. They may come back any minute."

"'They'? What do you mean?"

"Last night I heard noises coming from the garage. I went outside. There was a car with its headlights shining into the garage, and I could hear two men talking."

"Did you hear what they said?"

"Some of it, doc. But I couldn't get too near. I didn't want them to see me. I did hear one of them say, 'Amiss can't land on Barle Moor. It's too wet.'"

"Who is Amiss?"

"A helicopter pilot, doc. It's true!" Dave was excited.

"Did they say where he'll land instead?" Andrew asked.

"Yes — on Brockley Moor. That's twenty miles away!"

"Did you see the two men?"

"No. They stayed in the garage. But I'll tell you something, doc. I'm sure one of the men was Tom. I recognized his voice."

"What about the car?"

"It looked like a Rolls."

"They didn't go into the house?"

"No. They stayed in the garage."

"Dave, the police will want to know all this."

Dave jumped back. "Then *you'll* have to tell it to them, doc. I'm not coming."

"What are you going to do, then?"

"Stay here, of course."

"Why?"

"To see what happens."

"It may be dangerous, Dave."

"Don't worry, doc. They'll never catch me in these woods."

"You know I'll have to tell the police you're here?"

"You can tell them what you like, doc." He pointed to a fallen tree that had come down in the storm. It was just inside the wood. Its leaves were still green. "That's where I'll be. I can see the garage from there, but they'll never see me."

He started to run. Then he turned round. "I'll be there, doc. I promise."

He disappeared into the woods. Andrew looked inside the garage. It was empty. Then he drove to Dunsford police station and told the inspector everything that Dave had told him. He also told the inspector about the meetings between Oakley and Tom Cobley at Havercombe.

"Do you believe the boy, Dr. Fairbanks?" the inspector asked.

"Yes, I do."

"Interesting," the inspector said. "We know all about Cobley. But Oakley and Amiss? They must be smugglers. I'll phone Scotland Yard. They may know something about them . . . . ."

A few minutes later he came back. "No, they know nothing."

"What do you think the helicopter will carry?" Andrew asked.

"It's difficult to say. It might be drugs."

He went to a map on the wall and put his finger on Brockley Hill.

"I guess Cobley will meet the helicopter with his Land Rover here — this is the only place where a helicopter could land. Then he'll take what it's carrying to Woodlands House. Oakley will meet him there with his Rolls."

"What about the boy? Will he be in danger?" Andrew asked.

"He'll be all right if he keeps quiet and doesn't move."

"He won't move. But I'm the only person that knows where he's hiding."

The inspector smiled. "Are you asking to come with us?"

"I'll be very disappointed if I don't come with you!"

"Fine! But you're not a policeman, remember. If there's any shooting or fighting, just look after the boy, and don't let them see you. We'll fetch you at about eight o'clock."

Andrew went home and told Caroline. She was worried.

"Do you think they'll have guns, Andy?"

"I hope not!" Andrew said.

Suddenly she turned and looked at him. "Andy! You've known about Oakley and Cobley for days, and you've never said a word to me, not even when Oakley dislocated his shoulder!"

He laughed.

"Stop laughing, Andy! It wasn't fair."

"Well, suppose I'd been wrong? I can just see *you* laughing!"

Andrew spent the next two hours visiting his patients and then went into Dunsford for the evening surgery. As he drove home the sky was black with storm clouds. It was 7 o'clock when he reached home. Caroline was in the kitchen.

"I'm preparing you a really good supper tonight."

"So I won't die with an empty stomach?"

"That's right!"

They sat down at the kitchen table. Caroline was quieter than usual.

"You're a good cook — when you want to be!" Andrew said.

She looked at her watch. "They'll be here any minute," she said.

He took her hand. "Don't be so anxious, Caro!"

"Well, so many horrible things happen these days."

The front door bell rang.

Chapter 19

It had rained heavily between six and eight o'clock. But when Andrew got into the police car, the rain stopped. The sky became clear, and there was a moon.

"A perfect night for a helicopter trip," the inspector said.

"Have you any idea where the helicopter is coming from?" Andrew asked.

"From France, probably."

"What are your plans?"

"One of our cars will follow the Land Rover from Brockley Hill to Woodlands House. We will be at Woodlands House to meet them!"

As they were approaching Woodlands House, there was a radio message from the police car on Brockley Hill.

"01 to 09. The Land Rover is driving on to Brockley Hill. We can hear the helicopter. It's approaching fast."

"09 to 01," the inspector replied. "Follow the Land Rover as arranged. Keep out of sight. And don't let the helicopter pilot see you. He may have radio contact with Oakley."

A moment later they turned into a lane which ran behind some woods. As they got out of the car, it began to rain heavily again. The inspector turned to his men.

"We are now behind Woodlands House. You all know what to do."

He opened a gate and they entered the wood. He pointed to Andrew's black bag.

"I see you've come well prepared!" he said.

They walked one behind the other down the path,

the inspector leading. The rain poured down. It got under Andrew's shirt collar and dripped down his back. His shoes leaked. They found a place out of the rain near the back door.

"They won't see us or hear us in the rain," the inspector said. "Any questions? ..... All right, go to your positions. Follow the walls of the house, and you won't get lost. Report to me if you see anything suspicious. But you must not, I repeat, *not* let them see you until I blow my whistle."

The men disappeared into the dark. The inspector turned to Andrew.

"Find the boy, please, doctor. He may have some news. If he has, please bring it me. You're sure you can trust him?"

"Completely."

"Good. But remember, doctor, this is a police job. We don't want any dead heroes."

At that moment a policeman came to report. He had seen a light on in the garage.

"Show me!" the inspector said. Then he turned to Andrew. "I hope you find that boy, doctor. After a whole day in the rain, he may need something from your black bag!"

He disappeared with the policeman. It was very dark, but the light from the garage helped Andrew find the edge of the wood. He looked for the fallen tree, but inside the wood everything was black. Suddenly he felt a hand on his raincoat.

"Hey, doc! It's me."

Andrew crept under the leaves and sat down beside Dave.

"Are you all right?" he asked.

"Yes. Can you guess what's in the garage?"

"A Rolls Royce?"

"No. A large van. A man drove it here. He didn't drive well. He nearly hit the side of the garage. Then I saw he had his left arm in a sling."

"Where is he now?"

"In the garage."

"Is anyone with him?"

"No, he's alone. Why don't we go and catch him, doc? He's a lot older than you, and he can't use his left arm."

"No. That's a job for the police, Dave. They're hiding all round the house. Anyway, we've got to wait for the Land Rover and find out what's in it."

"Will they catch Tom?"

"Yes. He won't be able to get away."

Dave was silent.

"I must go and tell the inspector about the van. I'll be back. Stay here. Promise not to move."

"O.K., doc. You can trust me."

"I nearly forgot," Andrew said. "Here's an apple and a packet of biscuits. Enjoy yourself!"

He found the inspector and gave him the news.

"Oakley with a van? It's something fairly big, then. It won't be drugs. Thank you, doctor. Go back to the boy — oh, and tell him he's been very helpful."

The rain was getting less heavy and soon it stopped completely. Andrew crept under the leaves again and sat down beside Dave.

"Look!" Dave whispered.

Chapter 20

Oakley came out of the garage. He looked up at the dark sky and began to walk up and down. Every few minutes he looked at his watch. Finally he stopped and cried out, "What the hell's he doing?" Then he began to walk towards the road. They could no longer see him, and soon they could no longer hear him.

"Why don't they do something, doc?" Dave said.

"He'll come back, don't worry."

At that moment there was the sound of a car approaching. It's headlights shone on Oakley, who was running in front of it.

"It's Tom's Land Rover," Dave said. "I know those lights. One of them's brighter than the other."

The Land Rover stopped in front of the house. Oakley opened the car door. The man in the driving-seat was groaning.

"Why are you so late?" Oakley shouted. "What's the matter with you? Get out!"

Tom did not move. "You're lucky I got here at all," he said. "It's my foot. I can't stand on it."

"What's wrong with your foot? You mean you won't be able to drive the van?"

"No, I won't. You'll have to drive it yourself."

"You know quite well I can't drive the van to Birmingham with my arm in a sling."

"Well, you'll have to, because I can't drive anywhere with this foot."

Suddenly Oakley stretched out his right arm and pulled Tom from the driving-seat. Tom fell to the ground and roared with pain. He swore at Oakley.

"Quiet, you idiot!" Oakley said.

"What's the matter with him, doc?"

"Gout! That's what he had the night I came to see him at the farm. He refused to take the pills, and now look at him!"

Oakley pulled Tom to his feet.

"Mind my foot!" Tom howled.

"To hell with your foot! Go and open the back of the Land Rover. If you don't —"

At that moment a whistle blew. Policemen rushed out of the dark. Two of them took Oakley by the arm and led him to the back of the Land Rover.

"Open it!" one of them said.

"Ask Cobley," Oakley said. "It's his Land Rover."

A police car arrived. It stopped behind the Land Rover and four policemen jumped out. There were policemen everywhere. The lights of the police car lit up the scene. Tom Cobley lay on the ground, groaning. A policeman pulled him to his feet.

"The key!" he said. "Come on. Quick!"

Tom Cobley swore at him and threw the key on the ground. The policeman opened the door. There was a moment's silence. The policeman looked astonished. Then he turned to the inspector.

"They're people, sir. They've got dark skins."

"Who would have thought it!" the inspector said. "Illegal immigrants! I didn't expect that — not in this part of the country."

Andrew and Dave were standing just behind him. "Illegal immigrants? What does that mean?" Dave asked.

"They've come to Britain to get work," the inspector said. "Some of them may have their families here. But they need permits, and they haven't got them."

"I feel sorry for them," Andrew said.

"I agree," the inspector replied. "But the law's the law. Get them out!" he shouted to the policemen.

"Out!" one of the policemen said. Nothing happened. "They won't move, sir."

"They probably can't understand English," the inspector said. "But get them out!"

The policeman took the nearest man by the collar and pulled him out. That made them understand. They climbed out and stood in a row beside the Land Rover. They began to speak in their own language. They were shivering, and one of them never stopped coughing.

"What do you think they're saying, doc?" Dave asked.

"They're probably saying, 'Why did we come to this awful island where it rains all the time, and where they treat us like criminals.' "

Meanwhile the inspector stopped in front of each man and looked at him closely.

"They don't look too well, Dr. Fairbanks," he said. "Will you please come and have a look at them? You know thousands of people are dying of cholera where they come from?"

"Yes, I know that. But I can't find out whether they've got cholera just by looking at them. They'll have to have tests in one of the city hospitals."

"Will they be able to stay here if they haven't got cholera?" Dave asked.

"No, son," the inspector said. "They'll almost certainly have to go home again. Now, don't ask any more questions. There's work to do. Mason, Edwards! Get Oakley and Cobley into the car and drive them to the police station! Now, doctor!"

Andrew moved along the line of immigrants, looking closely at their eyes and skin. He reached the last one, a little man about thirty years old. He looked extremely ill. His eyes were half closed and he coughed almost without stopping. Andrew put out his arms and caught him just as he was about to fall.

* * *

Chapter 21

The police car stopped outside the doctor's house. Andrew got out and took the boy by the arm.

"You're coming with me, Dave."

"Thank you very much for your help, Dr. Fairbanks," the inspector said, "and thank you, too, son. Come and see me tomorrow morning. I want to talk to you. No! You needn't be afraid. I'm just going to give you some advice. That's all."

"I'll phone the city hospital tomorrow morning," Andrew said. "I'm fairly sure that man's got T.B."

"I'll send a man to see Mrs. Cobley," the inspector said. "He'll tell her that the boy's staying with you tonight."

The police car drove off and Andrew and Dave went into the house. Caroline came to meet them.

"Dave, this is my wife. Caroline, this is Dave!"

Dave's clothes dripped on the carpet. He stood there not knowing what to say. Caroline put her arm round his shoulders.

"You must have a hot bath at once, Dave. I don't know what we can do about clothes. My husband's are rather too big, and our son's are rather too small! But we'll manage."

She took Dave upstairs. A few minutes later she came down again.

"Darling, you should get out of your wet clothes, too. Go into the kitchen. I'll bring you a towel and some dry things." She stopped at the bottom of the stairs. "So nobody was hurt?"

"Nobody," Andrew said, "except a dozen illegal immigrants. Heaven knows how much they paid Oakley! And Oakley will only get about two years in prison for it."

"What about Tom Cobley?"

"He'll get less."

Half an hour later they were all sitting round the kitchen table drinking hot soup. Caroline had driven to a neighbour and borrowed some clothes for Dave.

"Well, Dave," Andrew said at last. "What are we going to do with you? You've helped to save a girl's life, and you've helped to catch a criminal. But you've run away from home, and you've nowhere to go."

"Yes, I have. I'll go back to the farm and look after Aunt Sybil."

"And spend your nights poaching?"

"That's not exciting any more!"

"What will you do when your uncle comes back?" Caroline asked.

"When I'm sixteen and can leave school, I'll go to the city."

Andrew looked surprised. "I thought you liked the country?"

"I do, but it's in the cities you get the excitement, isn't it? Hey, doc! What happened to the girl? I want to see her."

"She wants to see you. She's not on the phone. Take

my bike. You can go over and see her after tomorrow you've seen the inspector."

The telephone rang. Caroline answered it.

"Is it really serious?" She looked at Andrew and sighed. "I'll tell him, Mr. Bassett ..... It's about Mrs. Bassett," she said. "Her baby is arriving any minute."

Andrew got up.

"He'll come at once, Mrs. Bassett," Caroline said.

* * *

Questions

Chapter 1

1 What did Caroline and Mrs. Cobley say to one another on the phone?
2 What was the first thing that the boy said to the doctor?
3 Did Sybil Cobley know that the boy had had an accident? 'No, she .....' Complete the sentence.
4 Why didn't the boy feel any pain while the doctor was sewing up his arm?
5 How does Caroline spend her time when she's not looking after her husband and her son?

Chapter 2

1 If you hurt yourself badly, where do you go?
2 What was Tom Cobley doing in the waiting-room?
3 Why did Tom Cobley fall?
4 Why didn't Dave let his aunt know that he was going to ride a horse?
5 Why did Dave let Mrs. Cobley bandage his arm this time?

Chapter 3

1 Why did Dave try to run away?
2 Give a short description of Geoffrey Maxwell?
3 Why did Dr. Maxwell visit the Cobleys?
4 Why did Tom Cobley go to prison?
5 Where was Caroline when Andrew returned?

Chapter 4

1 Why was Mrs. Cobley almost crying when she phoned Andrew?
2 What did Mr. Walesby want when he phoned Andrew?
3 What does 'I'll see if my husband's in' mean?

4 Why did Andrew send Mr. Walesby to a doctor in London?
5 Does Mr. Walesby spend most of his time feeding his cats, sitting in his chair, lying in bed?

Chapter 5

1 Why was it so difficult walking across the moor?
2 How did Dave know the girl hadn't fallen off a horse?
3 Why can't the girl remember her name?
4 What happened on the way back to the car?
5 Why did Andrew let Dave walk in front of him?

Chapter 6

1 Why wasn't the car there?
2 Why did the car only travel a few yards?
3 When Andrew phones the hospital, what does he tell the sister?
4 Why is Andrew so grateful to Geoffrey Maxwell?
5 Why does Dave go on midnight trips with his uncle?

Chapter 7

1 Why won't Dave be afraid to answer questions at an inquest?
2 Who looks after Tom Cobley's farm?
3 How does Tom Cobley show that he's angry with Dave?
4 Why does Andrew wait for a while after Tom Cobley shuts the door?
5 What was Caroline busy doing when Andrew got home?

Chapter 8

1 When had Mr. Walesby had his last heart attack?
2 Why did Andrew never complain about the cats?
3 Did Mr. Walesby receive many letters? (answer using pronoun)

4 The housekeeper found something which surprised her. What was it?
5 Why did Mr. Walesby live all alone in this lonely house?

Chapter 9

1 What did he do as he ran down the passage?
2 How did Andrew know that Mr. Walesby was dead?
3 Why had Andrew arrived too late?
4 Why was it necessary to have a post-mortem?
5 What did Andrew expect to find on the desk?

Capter 10

1 Why does the detective want a written report from the doctor?
2 Why does Caroline guess that something is the matter?
3 Where did Andrew have his supper?
4 Why was Jennifer alone in the cottage?
5 When Andrew went to the hospital on the third day, what did he find?

Chapter 11

1 How did Jennifer find out where Mr. Walesby lived?
2 What did Mr. Walesby say when Jennifer phoned him?
3 Jennifer thinks that Mr. Walesby probably lied to her. Why?
4 What did Jennifer send to Mr. Walesby, and what did she write?
5 Why was Mrs. Martindale so anxious?
6 What is 104° in Centigrade (Celsius)?

Chapter 12

1 What jobs do Mr. and Mrs. Martindale do?
2 Explain, 'the river had burst its banks'.
3 Why couldn't Andrew drive to the hotel?
4 Why will Bridget have to go to hospital in the city?

8 Why will Bridget get better treatment at the city hospital?

Chapter 13

1 What does Andrew do to Bridget before the ambulance arrives?
2 Why does Andrew want Mrs. Martindale to go to the hospital with Bridget?
3 Who does Andrew write the letter to?
4 What interesting news does Dick Martindale give Andrew?
5 How will Mrs. Martindale let her husband know how Bridget is?
6 What did Andrew notice as he drove out of the village?
7 What surprise does Caroline get when Andrew arrives home?
8 What will Mike have to put up with?

Chapter 14

1 Why did Dave run away?
2 Was Dave wearing any shoes? (use pronoun in your answer)
3 What caused the bruises on Dave's back?
4 The social worker says, 'I agree with you'. Who does she agree with, and about what?
5 Why was Jennifer going to look for another job?
6 Why wasn't Jennifer sad when she heard her father had died?
7 Andrew didn't leave the hospital at once. Why?
8 What makes Andrew think that Jennifer will be rich?

Chapter 15

1 Why are there crowds in the town?
2 Why did Dave run away, do you think?
3 Andrew is working too hard. What does Caroline suggest that he does?
4 Why was the river so full?

5 Why was Dave surprised that Andrew caught a salmon?
6 Why can Dave guess what the moors are like in the winter?
7 Give two reasons why Dave came to see Andrew.
8 Why didn't Dave accept Andrew's invitation?

Chapter 16

1 Explain, 'Jennifer was as pale as ever'.
2 Why didn't Andrew take Jennifer into the living-room?
3 Why didn't Andrew tell Jennifer where Dave was?
4 Why did Andrew leave the room?
5 Why did Jennifer ask for a cloth?
6 Did Jennifer and Dave know each other?
7 Why did Andrew run down the road?

Chapter 17

1 Who got to the scene of the accident first?
2 Why was the accident Oakley's fault?
3 What did Andrew say to Oakley?
4 Oakley was in a hurry, so what did Andrew do?
5 How did Oakley pay the garage man?
6 How did Andrew eat his bread and cheese?
7 Why does Andrew wonder where Oakley is going?
8 Who does Andrew expect to see when he turns round?

Chapter 18

1 Dave tells Andrew he mustn't stay. Why?
2 How does Dave know that one of the men was Tom Cobley?
3 Why did Dave jump back?
4 Why did the police inspector phone Scotland Yard?

Chapter 19

1 What message did the police on Brockley Hill send to the inspector?
2 Why mustn't the police let the helicopter pilot see them?
3 Why does the inspector tell his men to follow the walls of the house?
4 What did the policeman report to the inspector?
5 How did Andrew and Dave find one another?
6 Why have they got to wait for the Land Rover?
7 Did Andrew give Dave any food? (answer using a pronoun)
8 What did Andrew tell Dave when he got back to him?

Chapter 20

1 Who was Oakley talking about when he said, "What the hell's he doing"?
2 Why couldn't Tom move?
3 Why couldn't Oakley stretch out his left arm?
4 What did Oakley tell Tom Cobley to do?
5 What was Tom doing, lying on the ground?
6 Why was the inspector surprised?
7 Why couldn't the policemen and the illegal immigrants talk to one another?
8 What was the last man in the line doing?

Chapter 21

1 Why did the inspector thank Dave?
2 Who let Mrs. Cobley know what had happened?
3 Why couldn't Dave wear Timothy's clothes?
4 Had anybody been hurt?
5 What were they all doing, sitting round the kitchen table?
6 Why does Dave want to live in the city?
7 What did Mr. Basset tell Caroline?
8 Do you think a doctor's life is interesting? If so, why? If not, why not?

Vocabulary

Italics = recognition vocabulary

to ache	[eik]	to hurt: my tooth **aches.**
alive	[ə'laiv]	not dead: you have to eat to stay **alive.**
all right	['ɔl'rait]	here: quite well, good
anaesthetic	[ænis'θetik]	
(local —)	['ləukl]	*(örtliche Betäubung)*
anti-tetanus	['ænti'tetənəs]	*(Anti)tetanus(spritze)*
attack	[ə'tæk]	When you become ill, you have an **attack** of . . . . . (the illness)
back	[bæk]	here: to go **back** etc. = to where you have come from
back door	['bæk'dɔː]	the door at the back of the house
bedclothes	['bedkləuðz]	the sheets and blankets on an English bed
bent	[bent]	to bend: my fork isn't straight — it's **bent**! Someone has **bent** it!
Bradford	['brædfəd]	town in the north of England
to breathe	[briːð]	You **breathe** through your nose and your mouth. There is too much smoke in here: I can't **breathe**!
breathing	[briːðiŋ]	I can't see you but I know you're there! I can hear you **breathing**!
bruise	[bruːz]	When you hurt your arm or your leg and it looks black and blue afterwards, you have a **bruise.**
can	[kæn]	= tin
cancer	['kænsə]	a very bad illness *(Krebs)*

casualty ward	['kæʒjuəlti 'wɔːd]	People who have had an accident go to the **casualty ward** when they arrive at the hospital *(Unfallstation)*
chest	[tʃest]	here: part of your body: the top of your body at the front
cholera	['kɔlərə]	*(Cholera)*
companion	[kəm'pæniən]	someone who is with you; someone who accompanies you
concussed	[kən'kʌst]	When you hit your head very hard and afterwards do not know what is happening, you are **concussed**,
concussion	[kən'kʌʃən]	what you have when you are concussed *(Gehirnerschütterung)*
couch	[kautʃ]	here: doctor's **couch**: what you sometimes have to lie down on when you visit the doctor
to cough	[kɔf]	When you have a **cough** and make a noise, you are **coughing.**
to cry (out) **to give a cry**	[krai]	to shout
day off	['dei 'ɔf]	a day when you don't have to work
depression	[di'preʃən]	a very sad feeling
disappointment	[disə'pɔintmənt]	I'm very disappointed. What a **disappointment**!
to dislocate	['disləkeit]	to pull out of place: when you **dislocate** your shoulder, the bone is out of place and it hurts!
to dress (a wound)	[dres]	to bandage; to put bandages on the place where you've cut yourself

driving-seat	['draiviŋ siːt]	the seat in a car where the driver sits
drugs	[drʌgz]	1. medicine *(Medikamente)* 2. *(Drogen)*
duty doctor	['djuːti'dɔktə]	the doctor whose turn it is to work, to be on **duty**
to empty	['empti]	to make empty
epidemic	[epi'demik]	When a lot of people in the same place get the same illness, we call it an **epidemic.**
to find out	['faind'aut]	to discover, to learn about sth.
fisherman	['fiʃəmən]	a man who catches fish
to forgive	[fə'giv]	When someone does something wrong and you say "It doesn't matter", you **forgive** him/her.
fracture	['fræktʃə]	When you break your arm or another bone, the doctor says you have a **fracture** of the arm etc.
fractured	['fræktʃəd]	= broken
garage man	['gærɑːʒ 'mæn]	He is usually a man who repairs cars.
gout	[gaut]	*(Gicht)*
headlight	['hedlait]	the main lights on a car at the front
health	[helθ]	When you are healthy you enjoy good **health**: when you are ill, your **health** is bad.
Health Service	['helθ'səːvis]	In Britain nearly all doctors belong to the (**National**) **Health Service.** You don't have to pay the doctor or the hospital.
heart	[hɑːt]	Your **heart** sends your blood round your body.
heart attack	['hɑːtə'tæk]	*(Herzinfarkt)*

hell!	[hel]	
to hell with...		English people often say this when they are angry. (Hell = *Hölle*)
housekeeper	['hauskiːpə]	a person who looks after a house, who cleans the house, does the shopping etc.
illegal immigrants	[iliːgəl 'imigrənts]	people who come into a country although they are not allowed to
illness	['ilnis]	He is very ill. He has a very bad **illness.**
to infect	[in'fekt]	*(infizieren)*
inquiries	[in'kwaiəriz]	When you ask a lot of questions about something, you are making **inquiries.** You make **inquiries** about the time a train arrives, for example.
jaws	[dʒɔːz]	the bones in your mouth that hold your teeth: you have to move them to eat your food
jeans	[dʒiːnz]	a kind of trousers
kid	[kid]	= child
Land Rover	['lænd'rəuvə]	a sort of car: the engine drives all four wheels. You can drive it on bad or difficult roads.
law	[lɔː]	You mustn't do that! It's against the **law.** *(das Gesetz)*
to leave	[liːv]	here: to give to someone when you die: when I die, I'm going to **leave** you all my money. It will all be yours.
to leave behind	['liːv bi'haind]	When you go away and forget to take something with you, then you have **left it behind.**
to light up	['lait 'ʌp]	to become bright, to make bright

to lock up	['lɔk 'ʌp]	All the doors are locked. Someone has **locked up.**
lock-jaw	[lɔk'dʒɔː]	= tetanus
long	[lɔŋ]	20 years is a **long** time.
lower	['ləuə]	= not as high, not as tall: the Matterhorn is **lower** than Mount Everest.
Mini	[mini]	kinds of British car
MG	['em'dʒiː]	
moor	['muə]	(Heide)
moorland	['muə'lænd]	
mirror	['mirə]	You can see your face in a **mirror.** You use a **mirror** in a car to see behind you.
mousy	['mausi]	like a mouse
mouse-coloured	['maus'kʌləd]	having the colour of a mouse
nephew	['nevjuː]	Your **nephew** is your brother's or your sister's son.
to park	[pɑːk]	to **park** a car = to leave a car somewhere, usually in a parking space
patient	['peiʃənt]	someone who is ill
to pay a visit	['pei ə 'vizit]	= to visit
penicillin	[peni'silin]	*(Penicillin)*
permit	['pəːmit]	You need a **permit** to buy a gun and you need a **permit** to go and live in another country.
to phone	[fəun]	= to tele**phone**
phone-box	['fəunbɔks]	= tele**phone**-box: you go into a **telephone box** to phone someone *(Telefonzelle)*
pill	[pil]	a kind of medicine: the doctor gives you **pills**: you have to take them every day when you are ill.

pillow	['piləu]	a cushion in bed: you put your head on it
pleurisy	['pluərisi]	a very bad illness: *(Brustfell-entzündung)*
poaching	['pəutʃiŋ]	killing wild animals without a permit (wildern)
pony	['pəuni]	*(Pony)* a small horse
pool	[pu:l]	a deep place in a river where the water moves slowy
post-mortem	['pəust] 'mɔ:təm]	When someone dies, a doctor has to examine the body to find out why he/she has died. This is a **post-mortem.**
practice (doctor's)	['præktis]	*(Praxis)*
prescription	[pris'kripʃən]	When a doctor wants to give you some medicine, he writes it down on a piece of paper which you have to take to a chemist. This is a **prescription.** *(Rezept)*
pneumonia	[nju'məunjə]	a very bad illness (Lungen-entzündung)
radio contact	['reidiəu 'kɔntækt]	When two people are in **radio contact**, they both have a radio and can speak to each other.
to recognize	['rekəgnaiz]	to know what or who sth. or s.o. is when you see it/him/her again: I **recognize** you. I've seen you before.
receptionist	[ri'sepʃənist]	the person you talk to first when you visit a doctor, or go into a hotel etc.
relation	[ri'leiʃən]	Here: a member of the same family *(Verwandte[r])*
rheumatism	['ru:mətizm]	an illness *(Rheumatismus)*

roar	[rɔː]	a loud noise: an engine roars, it makes a **roar**, it makes a loud noise
salmon	['sæmən]	*(Lachs)*
Scotland Yard	['skɔtlənd 'jɑːd]	(New) Scotland Yard is the main building of the London police. Scotland Yard detectives have become famous in most parts of the world.
serious	['siəriəs]	a **serious** accident = a very bad accident
to share	[ʃɛə]	to give someone part of something which you have: you **share** a bar of chocolate with someone = you give him/her a piece of it.
to shiver	['ʃivə]	When you are very cold, your body shakes. You **shiver** sometimes when you are frightened.
sister (hospital)	['sistə]	*(Oberschwester)*
silk	[silk]	*(Seide)*
sling	[sliŋ]	here: a kind of bandage: you put your arm in a **sling** when it is broken. It hangs round your neck.
smuggler	['smʌglə]	*(Schmuggler)*
social worker	['səuʃəl 'wəːkə]	someone who helps people with problems *(Sozialarbeiter)*
solicitor	[sə'lisitə]	*(Rechtsanwalt)*
splash	[splæʃ]	If you throw a stone into a river, it makes a **splash** in the water.
stable (riding)	['steibl]	You keep horses in a **stable.**
to swear (at)	[swɛə]	If you say "Oh hell!" when you are angry, then you are **swearing.**

steep	[stiːp]	difficult to climb: the Eiger or the Matterhorn are very **steep** mountains. Lorries drive very slowly up **steep** hills.
stitch	[stitʃ]	When you sew something you make **stitches** with a needle and cotton.
surgery	[ˈsəːdʒəri]	1. where the doctor sees his patients *(Praxis)* 2. the time when patients come to see the doctor *(Sprechstunde)*
stomach	[ˈstʌmək]	When you eat your food it goes into your **stomach.** *(Magen)*
swelling	[ˈsweliŋ]	If you hurt your arm and it gets bigger, then you have a **swelling** on your arm.
swollen	[ˈswəulən]	I've hurt my foot. It's **swollen**: I can't put my shoe on!
T.B.	[ˈtiːbiː]	the same in German!
temper	[ˈtempə]	Don't get angry! Don't lose your temper!
temperature	[ˈtempritʃə]	He is very ill. His **temperature** is 39° (degrees).
test	[test]	You have to have a **test** to find out what is wrong. You have a **blood-test** to find out if you are ill and why.
tetanus	[ˈtetənəs]	= lock-jaw *(Tetanus)*
thermometer	[θəˈmɔmitə]	You use this to take s.o.'s temperature
throat	[θrəut]	When you have a cold, your **throat** sometimes hurts. It hurts when you eat. The food goes through your mouth and down your **throat** (Hals) to your stomach.

tongue	[tʌŋ]	*(Zunge)* Your **tongue** is in your mouth. You use it for talking/or you talk with it.
to treat	[triːt]	If you are ill, the doctor has to **treat** you.
treatment	['tri'ːtmənt]	He gives you medicine and tells you to stay in bed. This is the best **treatment** for your illness. *(behandeln, Behandlung)*
trout	[traut]	a kind of fish *(Forelle)*
tyre	['taiə]	A car usually has four **tyres**: they are made of rubber. You keep a spare **tyre** in the back of the car.
ward (hospital)	[wɔːd]	a room in hospital where all the patients are in bed *(Station)*
whisky	['wiski]	a drink *(Whisky)*
whistle	['wisl]	In a football match you have to stop when you hear the **whistle**. *(Pfeife)*
wound	[wuːnd]	If you cut your arm, you have a **wound** in your arm.
to wound	[wuːnd]	to hurt, to cut, to injure
X-ray		If you break a bone in your body you have to have it **X-rayed**. You have to have an **X-ray**. *(Röntgenaufnahme)*

4 (1/4) Dr. Fairbanks 43541

Phrases

to get

to get back	When will you **get back**? When will you return?
to get started	Come on! Let's **get started**! Let's begin.
to get stuck	The car **got stuck** in the snow. We couldn't go any further.
to get s.o. into trouble	Don't talk to him! He's a criminal. He'll **get** you into **trouble**!
to get to	When will we **get to** London? When will we arrive?
to get away	She talked so much I couldn't **get away**. I couldn't leave.
to get on	I can't stop. I have to **get on**!
to get s.o. to do sth.	I can't mend it myself but I'll **get** someone else **to** mend it.
to get off	**Get off** my land! Go away!
to get paid	When do you **get paid**? At the end of the week.
to get in your eyes	I can't see. The rain **is getting in** my eyes.
to get out of	Come on! **Get out of** those wet clothes!
to get tired of	**I'm getting tired** of mending your bike every week! I'm fed up with it!
to get lunch	What time will you come home? Shall I **get lunch** for you at one o'clock?
to get to sleep	I'm not tired. I can't **get to sleep** at all.
to get better	Don't worry. You'll **get better** soon.
to get caught	Tom Cobley **got caught** by the police.
to get something finished	If you don't stop talking I'll never **get the job finished.**

to get lost	The old lady **got lost** in the fog.
to get s.th. moving	I can't **get** the car **moving**! Try pushing it!

to put

to put back	The doctor **put** his dislocated shoulder **back** (into place).
to put up with	I've **put up with** you for ten years, but now I'm leaving!
to put on weight	You've got heavier. You've **put on weight**!
to put on your brakes	Stop! **Put on the brakes**! Quick!
to put s.o. up	The hotels are all full. Who can **put us up** for the night?

to keep

to keep in	↔ to let out:
to keep hot	Your lunch **is keeping hot.**
to keep s.o. quiet	Your dog is barking. Can't you **keep him quiet**?
to keep your eyes on	Watch me all the time. **Keep your eyes on** me.
to keep s.o.	I won't **keep** you. You can go now.

Idiomatic Phrases

P. 9 Don't give the nurses any trouble.
P. 11 Are you in, Andy?
P. 20 I'll use the belt on you first.
P. 30 Mrs. Martindale is on the phone.
P. 39 The Patients had nothing wrong with them

GRADED READERS

eine Serie leicht zu lesender Lektüren mit zahlreichen Abbildungen
herausgegeben von Eric Orton

Series 1

Eric Orton: The Red Mini 43501

Ende 5. Schuljahr

„Sheila" ist verschwunden. Die Suche nach dem Dieb führt Jill und Clive Cooper zum Café auf der M 5. Der einzige Hinweis: der Mann hatte rotes Haar und eine ungewöhnliche Schuhgröße.

Series 1

Eric Orton: The Canal Tigers 43504

Ende 5. Schuljahr

Jim, Ginger, Pam und Penny dürfen in einem alten, leerstehenden Haus einen Jugendclub eröffnen. Die Kinder erleben seltsame Dinge in diesem Haus, und sie stoßen auf die "Canal Tigers" . . .

Series 2

Marianne Calmann: Red Light on the Tube 43503

ab 6. Schuljahr

Fußballfieber herrscht in London. Tony muß unbedingt zum Wembley-Stadion, doch unterwegs verliert er die Eintrittskarte. Dann sieht er zwei Leute in der U-Bahn mit *seiner* Tasche . . .

Series 3

Ted Cooke: Quintet up a Mountain 43502

ab 7. Schuljahr

Ferien im Gebirge Nordenglands für die Kinder aus der Stadt. Der waghalsige Charlie will ohne die Mädchen den Berg bezwingen. Er achtet nicht auf die Warnung. Der tückische Nebel bringt Gefahr. Charlie kommt nicht zurück. Kann Bill ihn noch aus der Gefahr retten?